FREEDOM

*A Daily Devotional
For those in the midst of the struggles of
life*

Tony Moore

Freedom
A Daily Devotional for those in the midst of the struggles of life.
Copyright © 2015
Moore & Associates, Inc.
6530 Sheridan Rd. Suite #3
www.mooreandassociates.biz
All rights reserved.

This book may not be copied or reprinted for commercial gain or profit. The use of short quotation or occasional page copying for personal or group study is permitted.

Published by: CreateSpace Independent Publishing Platform

First Printing, 2015
International Standard Book Number: 978-1508468431
Printed in the United States of America

For additional information, please contact:
Email: tmoore@mooreandassociates.biz
Tel: 262-605-1444
Fax: 262-605-1404

Cover Design and Page Layout by Angela Martinez, Digital Designs AM

Introduction

Tony Moore

There is a part of me that is looking to touch the world with the same knowledge that has been so freely given to me. Inside of me there lies all the potential of possibility, far greater than anything that I could ever have imagined. I once walked around a prison yard not knowing what I wanted to do with my life, not even knowing what led to me being in prison in the first place. At the same time, I always sensed that I was blessed with the knowledge that God touched me with a depth of realness that sometimes scares me. I went to juvenile prison at the tender age of 15, scared and ready to do battle with the all the demons found in prison. I had to become a fighter to survive that hell hole. I needed to do whatever it took to maintain some sort of respectability in the harsh reality of being away from Mom, Dad, and the family that I was missing. At those very moments of self-examination, I had to become what I thought a man should be.

One of the things about coming home from prison I had to realize is that all the effort to change would be up to me at first, because I had burned so many bridges in the past. I could not expect people I love to trust me enough to give me the support I would need to make a solid reentry into society. I knew that people would have a "wait and see" attitude concerning my change, because I had shared my story of transformation, after four other incarcerations, many times. This being my fifth release, the people I love must have thought "Why is this release any different?" For me it was different because I was different. I saw incarceration differently for the first time in my inmate career, which spanned over twenty five years, starting at the age of twelve years old and ending with my last incarceration at the age of thirty five. I became more focused on what I needed to do as a recovering addict to transform my life and reach my full potential as a man, father, ex-offender, and member of society. The one thing that made a lot of sense to me during my last incarceration was that God re-introduced himself to me, and I found a new understanding of the Bible and Jesus. I needed to have better self-discipline and self-control. So, as I read the Bible, I found that the Ten Commandments gave me a foundation to base my transformation and changes on.

As you reflect on the daily devotional message, use the lines that follow to capture your thoughts for that day. Reflect back on your thinking and personal growth as you move through the days.

Tony Moore

365 Daily Devotional

Day 1

I'm here in prison now.
I must stay committed to changing, so that I can get back home to my loved ones.

_____
_____
_____
_____
_____
_____

Day 2

"Examine yourselves as to whether you are in the faith; Test yourselves." - II Corinthians 13:5

_____
_____
_____
_____
_____
_____

Day 3

"We can change the way we think."

— Paul, an Apostle of Jesus Christ

_____
_____
_____
_____
_____
_____

Day 4

"Everyone thinks of changing the world, but no one thinks of changing himself." - Leo Tolstoy

_____
_____
_____
_____
_____
_____

Day 5

I must have the courage to envision what I want my change to look like.

_____
_____
_____
_____
_____

Day 6

"Who we are determines what we do." - John C. Maxwell

_____
_____
_____
_____
_____

Day 7

"Our thought determines our destiny. Our destiny determines our legacy." - James Allen

_____
_____
_____
_____
_____
_____

Day 8

I have to start the process of loving myself back to emotional health.

_____
_____
_____
_____
_____
_____

Day 9

"Positive thinking will let you do everything better than negative thinking will."- Zig Ziglar

_____
_____
_____
_____
_____
_____

Day 10

"Finish each day and be done with it. You have done what you could. Some blunders and absurdities no doubt crept in; forget them as soon as you can. Tomorrow is a new day. You shall begin it serenely and with too high a spirit to be encumbered with your old nonsense."
- Ralph Waldo Emerson

_____
_____
_____
_____
_____
_____

Day 11

Replace negative thoughts with productive thoughts that lead you to a productive outcome.

_____
_____
_____
_____
_____
_____

Day 12

Invest positive energy into the present instead of dwelling in the past on things you cannot change.

_____
_____
_____
_____
_____
_____

Day 13

"Good thoughts and action can never produce bad results; bad thoughts and action can never produce good results."
- James Allen

_____
_____
_____
_____
_____
_____

Day 14

"You have to think anyway, so why not think big."
- Donald Trump

_____
_____
_____
_____
_____
_____

Day 15

"People who go to the top think differently than others."
- William Arthur Ward

_____
_____
_____
_____
_____
_____

Day 16

I will be responsible today, for the choices are mine.

_____
_____
_____
_____
_____
_____

Day 17

Accountability is taking action consistent with a desired outcome.

_____
_____
_____
_____
_____
_____

Day 18

"Anything that is wasted effort represents wasted time. The best management of our time thus becomes linked inseparably with the best utilization of our efforts."

- Ted W. Engstrom

_____
_____
_____
_____
_____
_____

Day 19

"Let us not therefore judge one another anymore: but rather resolve this, not to put a stumbling block or a cause to fall in our brother's way." - Romans 14:13

_____
_____
_____
_____
_____
_____

Day 20

In your loneliness, seek and find your inner voice of reasoning. This is where you will find your moment of clarity for your situation.

_____
_____
_____
_____
_____
_____

Day 21

"There is no easy walk to freedom."- Nelson Mandela

_____
_____
_____
_____
_____
_____

Day 22

I have to be able to see myself as a free man before I can become one.

_____
_____
_____
_____
_____
_____

Day 23

"Liberty is the capacity to do anything that does no harm to others." - Declaration of the rights of man and the citizen, France, article 4, 1789

_____
_____
_____
_____
_____
_____

Day 24

The desire for your freedom is hidden in your daily routine.

_____
_____
_____
_____
_____
_____

Day 25

I have to pay attention to what really matters as it relates to my freedom.

_____
_____
_____
_____
_____
_____

Day 26

"Your freedom and mine cannot be separated."
- Nelson Mandela

_____
_____
_____
_____
_____
_____

Day 27

I have to build my freedom on a solid foundation.

_____
_____
_____
_____
_____
_____

Day 28

Change comes whether you want it to or not, so pick how you will embrace your change.

_____
_____
_____
_____
_____
_____

Day 29

"Those who prize freedom only for the material benefits it offers have never kept it for long." - Alexis de Tocqueville

_____
_____
_____
_____
_____
_____

Day 30

"Freedom - it is today more than ever the most precious human possession." - Pearl Buck

_____
_____
_____
_____
_____
_____

Day 31

When's the best time to get started? Now! As soon as you get the idea to act - act! Take the plunge! Strike while the iron's hot.

Day 32

Knowledge is power. I will start to discipline myself by reading something every day until I get out of jail.

Day 33

Ask somebody who is making it happen to educate you about this thing called life. Don't let your foolish pride block you from getting wisdom or knowledge, it's free.

Day 34

I must respect the people of this place because I'm a guest in their house.

Day 35

I will use this jail time to gain knowledge so that I will grow mentally, emotionally, and in my education.

Day 36

If you want knowledge you will have to read and study. If you want wisdom you will have to pray continuously.

Day 37

Today is the day I start to practice asking for help from God, jailers, family members, and inmates so that I can begin to understand what it is going to take to get out of prison and stay out of prison.

_____
_____
_____
_____
_____
_____

Day 38

Happy to know this is my last prison bit.

_____
_____
_____
_____
_____
_____

Day 39

"There is no more noble occupation in the world then to assist another human being; to help someone succeed."
— Alan Loy McGinnis

Day 40

"Let us therefore come boldly to the throne of grace that we may obtain mercy and find grace to help in time of need." - Hebrews 4:16

Day 41

One day at a time.

Day 42

Slow down, your season is coming.

Day 43

Maintaining focus and staying on track is hard in this place, but the reward of freedom outweighs all of the stress.

_____
_____
_____
_____
_____
_____

Day 44

"To keep your plans on track, create a timeline for all your major projects. Use it to establish objectives and deadlines for the accomplishment of each major step." - Unknown

_____
_____
_____
_____
_____
_____

Day 45

I will not let the loneliness of this prison cell stop me from hoping and dreaming of a brighter tomorrow.

Day 46

Oh, how I long to be in the arms of my mother.

Day 47

"It must be borne in mind that the tragedy of life doesn't lie in not reaching your goal. The tragedy lies in having no goal to reach. It isn't a calamity to die with dreams unfulfilled, but it is a calamity not to dream. It is not a disaster to be unable to capture your ideal, but it is a disaster to have no idea to capture. It is not a disgrace not to reach the stars, but it is a disgrace to have no stars to reach for. Not failure, but low aim is a sin."

- Benjamin E. Mayes

_____
_____
_____
_____
_____

Day 48

"There are those that look at things the way they are, and ask why? I dream of things that never were, and ask why not." - Robert F. Kennedy

_____
_____
_____
_____
_____

Day 49

Expect success rather than fear failure.

_____
_____
_____
_____
_____
_____

Day 50

"Nothing is as real as a dream. The world can change around you, but your dream will not. Responsibilities need not erase it. Duties need not obscure it. Because the dream is within you, no one can take it away."

- Tom Clancy

_____
_____
_____
_____
_____
_____

Day 51

Focus on solutions rather than remain stuck in the problem.

_____
_____
_____
_____
_____
_____

Day 52

"Successful people are successful because they form the habits of doing those things that failures don't like to do."
- Albert Gray

_____
_____
_____
_____
_____
_____

Day 53

"The elevator to success is out of order. You'll have to use the stairs... one step at a time." - Joe Girard

_____
_____
_____
_____
_____
_____

Day 54

If you want to be successful you have to practice what you studied, and have the wisdom to use your faith for what you have prayed for.

_____
_____
_____
_____
_____
_____

Day 55

"Without ambition one starts nothing. Without work one finishes nothing. The prize will not be sent to you. You have to win it. The man who knows how will always have a job. The man who also knows why will always be his boss. As to methods there may be a million and then some, but principles are few. The man who grasps principles can successfully select his own methods. The man, who tries methods, ignoring principles, is sure to have trouble."

— Ralph Waldo Emerson

Day 56

"Many of life's failures are people who did not realize how close they were to success when they gave up."

— Thomas A. Edison

Day 57

"Success often comes to those who have the aptitude to see way down the road." - Laing Burns, Jr.

_____
_____
_____
_____
_____
_____

Day 58

It's not what has happened to me in my past that motivates me to win. It is what God has put in me that motivates me to win. (Thank You, Jesus!)

_____
_____
_____
_____
_____
_____

Day 59

"Dwell not on the past. Use it to illustrate a point, and then leave it behind. Nothing really matters except what you do NOW in this instant of time. From this moment onwards you can be an entirely different person, filled with love and understanding, ready with an outstretched hand, uplifted and positive in every thought and deed."

- Eileen Caddy

_____
_____
_____
_____
_____
_____

Day 60

"Let us not seek to fix the blame for the past. Let us accept our own responsibility for the future." - John F. Kennedy

_____
_____
_____
_____
_____
_____

Day 61

Unless you can embrace your past experiences you will not be able to reap the benefits of the life lessons to teach future generations of your children.

Day 62

Always accept responsibility for your past behavior and how it affected others and learn from your mistakes.

Day 63

Overcome obstacles, slumps, or defeat with a renewed positive attitude.

_____
_____
_____
_____
_____

Day 64

"Our attitudes control our lives. Attitudes are a secret power working twenty-four hours a day, for good or bad. It is of paramount importance that we know how to harness and control this great force." - Tom Blandi

_____
_____
_____
_____
_____

Day 65

Enjoy life with a positive attitude and a passion for the future.

_____
_____
_____
_____
_____
_____

Day 66

If you want to become more positive in your life be around positive people.

_____
_____
_____
_____
_____
_____

Day 67

You must maximize your thinking about the positive thing that you want to bring about in your life.

_____
_____
_____
_____
_____
_____

Day 68

"Whatever failures I have known, whatever errors I have committed, whatever follies I have witnessed in private and public life have been the consequence of action without thought." - Bernard M. Baruch

_____
_____
_____
_____
_____
_____

Day 69

Remember to shake off failure and look at it in a positive light as you have a chance to improve upon the failure the next time around.

Day 70

"It's how you deal with failure that determines how you achieve success." - David Feherty

Day 71

Failure only means that I have tried again and I'm closer to my idea of success.

Day 72

If you are scared to do what you want to do in life because of fear, you will never have the courage to reach the untapped potential that lies within you; the gift that you are born with.

Day 73

"A Psalm of David. 'The LORD is my light and my salvation; whom shall I fear? The LORD is the strength of my life; of whom shall I be afraid." - Psalm 27:1

Day 74

Have the courage to confront and face your internal fears of inadequacies.

Day 75

"When failure is not an option, nothing serves a person better than to teach it thinking." - John C. Maxwell

_____
_____
_____
_____
_____
_____

Day 76

"Everyone has inside of him/her a piece of good news. The good news is that you don't know how great you can be! How much you can love! What you can accomplish! And what your potential is!" - Anne Frank

_____
_____
_____
_____
_____
_____

Day 77

You have the potential to succeed, but you're going to have to work the principles that you know will make you successful.

_____
_____
_____
_____
_____
_____

Day 78

Once you find the truth, it shall set you free internally so that you will know a new level of peace concerning your potential.

_____
_____
_____
_____
_____
_____

Day 79

Reaching your full potential is that thing that you always seek and practice with discipline. Strive for continuous perfection of those things that are within your GOD given gifts, or the talents that you have attained through life experiences; and lessons from others.

_____
_____
_____
_____
_____
_____

Day 80

Every day I ask myself and my clients, "Why haven't you reached your full potential?"

_____
_____
_____
_____
_____
_____

Day 81

There are levels you must understand before you practice releasing your potential.

Day 82

"Let no man say when he is tempted, 'I am tempted by God' For God cannot be tempted by evil, nor does He Himself tempt anyone." - James 1:13

Day 83

"But as it is written: Eye has not seen, nor ear heard, nor have entered into the heart of man, the things which God has prepared for those that love him." - I Corinthians 2:9

Day 84

"Yet; in all these things we are more than conquerors through Him who loved us." - Romans 8:37

Day 85

"For God so loved the world that he gave His only begotten Son, that whoever believes in Him should not perish but have everlasting life." - John 3:16

_____
_____
_____
_____
_____
_____

Day 86

"Jesus answered him, 'the first of all the commandments is: 'Hear, O Israel; the Lord our God, the Lord is one and you shall love the Lord your God with all your heart, with all your soul, with all your mind, and with all your strength.' This is the first commandment." - Mark 12:29-30

_____
_____
_____
_____
_____
_____

Day 87

"Love does no harm to a neighbor; therefore love is the fulfillment of the law." - Romans 13:10

_____
_____
_____
_____
_____
_____

Day 88

"Just don't give up trying to do what you really want to do. Where there is love and inspiration, I don't think you can go wrong." - Ella Fitzgerald

_____
_____
_____
_____
_____
_____

Day 89

"And we know that all things work together for good to those who love God, to those who are called according to His purpose." - Romans 8:28

_____
_____
_____
_____
_____
_____

Day 90

"The goal you set must be challenging. At the same time, it should be realistic and attainable, not impossible to reach. It should be challenging enough to make you stretch, but not so far that you break." - Rick Hansen

_____
_____
_____
_____
_____
_____

Day 91

"Finally, brethren, whatever things are true, whatever things are noble, whatever things are just, whatever things are pure, whatever things are lovely, whatever things are of good report, if there is any virtue and if there is anything praiseworthy – meditate on these things. Whatever things are true… noble… just… pure… lovely… are of good report, if there is any virtue and if there is anything praiseworthy; think on these things."
- Philippians 4:8, Paul, the Apostle

Day 92

Live without pretending, love without depending, listen without defending, and speak without offending.

Day 93

"Blessed is the man who endures temptation; for when he has been approved, he will receive the crown of life which the Lord has promised to those who love Him."

– James 1:12

Day 94

"I have decided to stick with love. Hate is too great a burden to bear." - Dr. Martin Luther King

Day 95

"Love worketh no ill to his neighbour: therefore love *is* the fulfilling of the law." - Romans 13:10

_____
_____
_____
_____
_____
_____

Day 96

God has given you so many gifts, to sow love and to give hope, to shine light and to spread joy.

_____
_____
_____
_____
_____
_____

Day 97

Your current situation is not your end result!

Day 98

My heart is heavy for a touch of love, but I will meditate on the goodness of GOD.

Day 99

I must find the tools that are available in this prison to help me rebuild my life.

Day 100

"You must look within for value, but must look beyond for perspective." -Denis Waitley

Day 101

"Rejoiceth not in iniquity, but rejoiceth in the truth."
                    -I Corinthians 13:6

Day 102

Hang in there sister and brother. It will get hard sometimes, but this is what has to happen when you're doing great work.

Day 103

"You will be as much value to others as you have been to yourself." - Marcus T. Cicero

Day 104

"The person with a plan, a picture, will go after thoughts that add value to their thinking." - John C. Maxwell

Day 105

"We've met the enemy, and he is us." Recognize that your major time waster is not someone or something else...it's you! "Value every precious minute in your day."

– Unknown

_____
_____
_____
_____
_____
_____

Day 106

"One of the most essential things you need to do for yourself is to choose a goal that is important to you. Perfection does not exist -- you can always do better and you can always grow." - Les Brown

_____
_____
_____
_____
_____
_____

Day 107

"Leaders aren't born, they are made. And they are made just like anything else, through hard work. And that's the price we'll have to pay to achieve that goal, or any goal."

- Vince Lombardi

_____
_____
_____
_____
_____
_____

Day 108

Time is your greatest ally! By taking action, you gain immediate control over your work, schedule, and goals. So stop putting it off and start now.

_____
_____
_____
_____
_____
_____

Day 109

"Goals are not only absolutely necessary to motivate us. They are essential to really keep us alive."

— Rev. Robert H. Schuller

_____
_____
_____
_____
_____
_____

Day 110

Always re-evaluate if your plan and goals fit within the time frame that you are working with.

_____
_____
_____
_____
_____
_____

Day 111

Always check your gauges of life to maintain your highest energy level to accomplish each goal you have set out to achieve.

Day 112

Have patience with your goals and have realistic expectations about the results of any endeavor that you are hoping to accomplish.

Day 113

"Until thought is linked with purpose there is no intelligent accomplishment." - James Allen

Day 114

As in any great accomplishment, to whom much is given, much is required.

Day 115

"If you want to make good use of your time, you've got to know what's most important and then give it all you've got." - Lee Iacocca

_____
_____
_____
_____
_____
_____

Day 116

"In truth, people can generally make time for what they choose to do; it is not really the time but the will that is lacking." - Sir John Lubbock

_____
_____
_____
_____
_____
_____

Day 117

"The idea is to make decisions and act on them - to decide what is important to accomplish, to decide how something can best be accomplished, to find time to work at it and to get it done." - Karen Kakascik

_____
_____
_____
_____
_____
_____

Day 118

"You will never FIND time for anything. If you want time, you must MAKE it." - Charles Bixton

_____
_____
_____
_____
_____
_____

Day 119

"Most people spend more time planning their summer vacation then planning their lives." - Unknown

Day 120

"Making it big takes hard work." - Kevin Hart

Day 121

"If your dream is a big dream, and if you want your life to work on the high level that you say you do, there's no way around doing the work it takes to get you there."
						- Joyce Chapman

_____
_____
_____
_____
_____
_____

Day 122

You must work on your freedom as though your life depends on it.

_____
_____
_____
_____
_____
_____

Day 123

Be prepared to work and succeed on your own merit. Don't allow yourself to feel that the world owes you anything.

_____
_____
_____
_____
_____

Day 124

"The real winners in life are the people who look at every situation with an expectation that they can make it work or make it better." - Barbara Pletcher

_____
_____
_____
_____
_____

Day 125

"Reschedule all your preoccupations today, and you'll eliminate the largest hindrance to your productivity."

- Unknown

Day 126

"Don't tell me how hard you work. Tell me how much you get done." - James Ling

Day 127

"Time is at once the most valuable and the most perishable of all our possessions." - John Randolph

_____
_____
_____
_____
_____
_____

Day 128

"Some self-confronting questions: Where do I want to be at any given time? How am I going to get there? What do I have to do to get myself from where I am to where I want to be? What's the first, small step I can take to get moving?" - George A. Ford

_____
_____
_____
_____
_____
_____

Day 129

"A journey of 1000 miles begins with the first step."
- Chinese proverb

Day 130

"Champions know there are no shortcuts to the top. They climb the mountain one step at a time. They have no use for helicopters!" - Judi Adler

Day 131

Today I will start by forgiving myself for leaving my family, my wife or husband, my boyfriend or girlfriend, and my children.

_____
_____
_____
_____
_____

Day 132

It is a joy to be free from jail for over twenty years and have such a beautiful family and supporting cast of friends, brothers and sisters in Christ. I'm motivated to go higher in God's will for my life.

_____
_____
_____
_____
_____

Day 133

I will not allow this prison to detour me from changing my outlook on my journey home.

Day 134

I must look at the man in the mirror today and ask him to change his ways.

Day 135

Unless you change how you are, you will always have what you got.

Day 136

You can listen to and read all of the self-development in the world, but if you don't put what you have learned into action, things won't change.

Day 137

"Be ye not unequally yoked together with unbelievers, for what fellowship hath righteousness with unrighteousness? And what communion hath light with darkness?"

- II Corinthians 6:14

_____
_____
_____
_____
_____
_____

Day 138

If you want massive changes in your life, you must make massive changes to your life.

_____
_____
_____
_____
_____
_____

Day 139

Change is all about movement and discomfort; don't allow the feelings and emotions to control you.

_____
_____
_____
_____
_____
_____

Day 140

"Let us therefore follow after the things which make for peace, and things wherewith one may edify another."
- Romans 14:19

_____
_____
_____
_____
_____
_____

Day 141

Lord, give unto me the peace that sleep brings to the soul.

___

Day 142

"Be ready when opportunity comes. Luck is the time when preparation and opportunity meet." - Roy D. Chapin Jr.

Day 143

Get over your guilt and celebrate the opportunity you have for a second chance to redeem your life from the pit of despair.

Day 144

"People wait for opportunity to come along... yet it is there every morning." - Dennis the Menace

Day 145

"Obstacles are necessary for success... as in all careers of importance, victory comes only after many struggles and countless defeats. Yet each struggle, each defeat, sharpens your skills and strengths, your courage and your endurance, your ability and your confidence and thus each obstacle is a comrade-in-arms forcing you to become better... or quit. Each rebuff is an opportunity to move forward; turn away from them, avoid them, and throw away your future." - Og Mandino

_____
_____
_____
_____
_____

Day 146

"Few people have any next, they live from hand to mouth without a plan, and are always at the end of their line."
 - Ralph Waldo Emerson

_____
_____
_____
_____
_____
_____

Day 147

"Take time every day to reflect back and plan forward."
- Unknown

_____
_____
_____
_____
_____
_____

Day 148

"A man/woman who does not think and plan long ahead will find trouble right at his door." – Confucius

_____
_____
_____
_____
_____
_____

Day 149

Like any good builder you must plan, prepare, and count the cost before starting any project.

Day 150

"The Lord is not slack concerning his promise, as some men count slackness; but is longsuffering to us-ward, not willing that any should perish, but that all should come to repentance." - 2 Peter 3:9

Day 151

"You may not control all of today's events, but you must control how you respond to them." - Unknown

Day 152

"Finish each day and be done with it. You have done what you could. Some blunders and absurdities no doubt crept in; forget them as soon as you can. Tomorrow is a new day; begin it well and serenely and with too high a spirit to be encumbered with your old nonsense."
- Ralph Waldo Emerson

Day 153

"You are today where your thoughts have brought you. You will be tomorrow where your thoughts take you."
- James Allen

_____
_____
_____
_____
_____
_____

Day 154

Stop and Think Things Through –
BEFORE Taking Action...

_____
_____
_____
_____
_____
_____

Day 155

When you act immediately, you free up future time to be ready for the next item.

Day 156

When your passion meets your energy and your energy meets your action your action will meet your results.

Day 157

"If your actions inspire others to dream more, learn more, do more and become more, you are a leader."
- John Quincy Adams

Day 158

"The actions of man are the best interpreters of their thoughts."   - John Locke

Day 159

When your passion meets your energy, and your energy meets your action, your action will meet your results.

Day 160

Dreams and vision are made through plans and action.

Day 161

"A plan is a list of actions arranged in whatever sequence is thought likely to achieve an objective."

- John Argenti

_____
_____
_____
_____
_____

Day 162

"I believe that any man/woman's life will be filled with constant and unexpected encouragement, if he makes up his mind to do his level best each day, and as nearly as possible reaching the high water mark of pure and useful living." - Booker T. Washington

_____
_____
_____
_____
_____
_____

Day 163

The same thing I used to get out of prison is the same thing I use to stay out of prison. MY BRAIN.

Day 164

"The most practical, beautiful, workable philosophy in the world won't work – if you won't." - Zig Ziglar

Day 165

"Nothing is more difficult, and therefore more precious, then to be able to decide." - Napoléon Bonaparte

_____
_____
_____
_____
_____
_____

Day 166

"It takes as much energy to wish as it does to plan."
— Eleanor Roosevelt

_____
_____
_____
_____
_____
_____

Day 167

"The difficulty lies not so much in developing new ideas as in escaping from the old ones." - John Maynard Keynes

Day 168

To gain your freedom is a great task, but to keep your freedom is the greatest feat of all.

Day 169

"Possession of the ball is the key to winning in football, basketball, and the game of life." - Laing Burns, Jr.

Day 170

"It is easy to get to the top after you get through the crowd at the bottom." - Zig Ziglar

Day 171

I have to get back to my children. I need to be consistent so that I develop the discipline necessary to stay free, internally and externally.

Day 172

Good things come to those who have patience and take consistent, persistent actions toward their dreams of freedom.

Day 173

Everything begins with a thought. "Life consists of what a man is thinking about all day." - Ralph Waldo Emerson

_____
_____
_____
_____
_____
_____

Day 174

"Success is to be measured not so much by the position one has reached in life as by the obstacles which he has overcome while trying to succeed."
- Booker T. Washington

_____
_____
_____
_____
_____
_____

Day 175

You must invest in the possibility of you regaining your freedom, and the possibility that you will succeed.

Day 176

Take charge of your life, you got the ball and now it is in your court.

Day 177

I have the choice to take charge of my life, so today I commit to that endeavor.

Day 178

"If one advances confidently in the direction of one's dreams, and endeavors to live the life which he has imagined, he will meet with a success unexpected in common hours." - Henry David Thoreau

Day 179

"Let every nation know, whether it wishes us well or ill, that we shall pay any price, bear any burden, meet any hardship, support any friend, oppose any foe to assure the survival and the success of liberty." – John F. Kennedy

Day 180

The problem that challenges you the most is the problem that will launch you into your future success.

Day 181

Your respect for time is a prediction of your future success.

Day 182

You must overcome the odds that may be against you by using spiritual principles to even the playing field and to gain success.

Day 183

Stay of good cheer, all great success requires tests, trials, and sacrifice.

Day 184

"Every successful man I have heard of has done the best he could with conditions as he found them."
— Edgar Watson Howe

Day 185

"It is never too late to be who you might have been."

- George Eliot

_____
_____
_____
_____
_____
_____

Day 186

"Effort only fully releases its reward after a person refused to quit." - Napoléon Hill

_____
_____
_____
_____
_____
_____

Day 187

I have to prepare myself for this race to regain my freedom at all cost.

Day 188

Remember that your breakthrough is only a day away. Continue to keep faith in what you have started and allow yourself to see through the eyes of a winner.

Day 189

Today I must keep my focus on change and my mind on the prize, my (freedom).

Day 190

"Freedom is fragile and must be protected. To sacrifice it, even as a temporary measure, is to betray it."

— Germaine Greer

Day 191

"If men and women are in chains anywhere in the world, their freedom is endangered everywhere."
- John F. Kennedy

Day 192

If you put in minimal effort, you get minimal results.

Day 193

You have not failed at life with any defeat until you have not even one ounce of effort to give.

Day 194

"Now unto him that is able to do exceeding abundantly above all that we ask or think, according to the power that worketh in us." - Ephesians 3:20, Paul, the Apostle

Day 195

You must see beyond your barriers that keep you from attaining the next level of success.

Day 196

"Nothing limits achievement like small thinking; nothing expands possibility like unleashed thinking."
- William Arthur Ward

Day 197

"People will never attain what they cannot see themselves doing." - Karen Ford

Day 198

"You will become as small as your controlling desire, as great as your dominant aspiration." – James Allen

Day 199

"The person with a fixed goal, a clear picture of his desire, or an ideal always before him, causes it, through repetition, to be buried deeply in his subconscious mind and is thus enabled, thanks to its generative and sustaining power, to realize his goal in a minimum of time and with a minimum of physical effort. Just pursue the thought unceasingly. Step by step you will achieve realization, for all your faculties and powers become directed to that end." - Claude M. Bristol

Day 200

"Nurture great thoughts, for you will never go higher in your thoughts." - Benjamin Disraeli

Day 201

Look to the future for the possibilities of greatness for the sake of humanity.

Day 202

"I don't know what my calling is, but I want to be here for a bigger reason. I strive to be like the greatest people who have ever lived." - Will Smith

Day 203

The greater the sacrifices, the greater the rewards.

Day 204

The greatest journey we can take is the one that takes us inward, to the depths of our own soul. When we find ourselves in our search inward, we can move forward against all odds.

Day 205

"For the flower to blossom, you need the right soil as well as the right seed. The same is true to cultivate good thinking." - William Bernbach

Day 206

Stay positive with your thinking. Don't let the issues of others dictate your emotions.

Day 207

"Keep your mind off the things you don't want by keeping it on the things you do want." - W. Clement Stone

_____
_____
_____
_____
_____

Day 208

You must push yourself, and you're thinking, to a new level of awareness every day.

_____
_____
_____
_____
_____

Day 209

"If you open yourself up to possibility thinking, you open yourself up to many other possibilities." - John C. Maxwell

Day 210

Never allow the size of the project to deter you from victory. Be of good report because you have already won the battle.

Day 211

How many projects do you have that are unfinished? That is unacceptable, do not wait another moment, get up and start doing one project at a time, TODAY.

Day 212

"The joy is in creating, not maintaining."
- Vincent Lombardi

Day 213

"You can't use up creativity. The more you use, the more you have." - Maya Angelou

_____
_____
_____
_____
_____
_____

Day 214

An uncommon vision always creates an uncommon result.

_____
_____
_____
_____
_____
_____

Day 215

"All human development, no matter what form it takes, must be outside the rules: otherwise, we would never have anything new." - Charles Kettering

_____
_____
_____
_____
_____

Day 216

"Most people are more satisfied with old problems than committed to finding new solutions." - John C. Maxwell

_____
_____
_____
_____
_____

Day 217

When your heart chooses a destination, your mind will create the map.

Day 218

The atmosphere you create determines the product you produce.

Day 219

"Men occasionally stumble over the truth, but most pick themselves up and hurry off as if nothing has happened."
— Winston Churchill

Day 220

"Before it can be solved, a problem must be clearly defined." - William Feather

Day 221

"The will to win is worthless if you do not have the will to prepare." - Thane Yost

Day 222

"The man who is prepared for his battle have fought."
                                       - Miguel de Cervantes

Day 223

"The unexamined life is not worth living." - Socrates

_____
_____
_____
_____
_____

Day 224

"A human being may be defined as a personality with a will of his own capable of making moral choices between good and evil." - Arnold J. Toynbee

_____
_____
_____
_____
_____

Day 225

"To doubt everything or to believe everything are two equally convenient solutions; both dispense with the necessity of reflection." - Jules Henri Poincaré

Day 226

"We are the choices we have made." - Meryl Streep

Day 227

I must unlock the potential that is buried in my soul, so that I can become all that God has made me to be.

Day 228

"The word impossible is not in my dictionary."
- Napoléon Bonaparte

Day 229

"We must stop assuming that a thing which has never been done before probably cannot be done it all."
- Donald M. Nelson

_____
_____
_____
_____
_____
_____

Day 230

"Be ashamed to die until you have won some victories for humanity." - Horace Mann

_____
_____
_____
_____
_____
_____

Day 231

"When you reflect, you are able to put an experience into prospective." - John C Maxwell

_____
_____
_____
_____
_____
_____

Day 232

I'm not an answering machine, I am a questioning machine. If we have all the answers, how come we're in such a mess?

_____
_____
_____
_____
_____
_____

Day 233

"To accept good advice is but to increase one's own ability." - Johann Wolfgang von Goethe

Day 234

"He that is taught only by himself has a fool for a master."
- Ben Jonson

Day 235

"Brave men earned the right to shape their own destiny."
- Arthur M. Schlesinger Jr.

_____
_____
_____
_____
_____
_____

Day 236

"Liberty consists in the ability to choose." - Simone Weil

_____
_____
_____
_____
_____
_____

Day 237

"To live is to choose. But to choose well, you must know who you are and what you stand for, where you want to go and why you want to get there." - Kofi Annan

_____
_____
_____
_____
_____
_____

Day 238

When you want something you've never had, you've got to do something you've never done.

_____
_____
_____
_____
_____
_____

Day 239

"Everyone has the right to a standard of living adequate for the health and well-being of himself and of his family, including food, clothing, and housing and medical care and necessary social services, and the right to security in the event of unemployment, sickness, disability, widowhood, old age or other lack of livelihood in circumstances beyond his control." - Universal Declaration of Human Rights

Day 240

What you permit to enter your life will determine what exits your life.

Day 241

Your rewards in life are determined by the visions you achieve.

_____
_____
_____
_____
_____
_____

Day 242

Your transformation and newness in life will transform your legacy for your children, and your children's children.

_____
_____
_____
_____
_____
_____

Day 243

This is the moment... when GOD lets you know that a change is about to come into your life, and the knowledge to know that you been preparing for this moment all your life.

Day 244

Don't allow resentments and grudges to blacken your heart. Always forgive quickly and often so that you can continue to move forward without pain.

Day 245

I believe in prayer and I'm asking that all of you, who pray in the name of JESUS, ask that GOD bless my situation in life and help me to be a better servant to his people.

Day 246

I will not complain about what I have permitted in my life.

Day 247

"So if you stay ready, you ain't gotta get ready, and that is how I run my life." - Will Smith

_____
_____
_____
_____
_____
_____

Day 248

If you know my story, you would know that I have already won.

_____
_____
_____
_____
_____
_____

Day 249

The size of your vision determines the size of your prize.

_____
_____
_____
_____
_____
_____

Day 250

"Not everyone can see the light of your vision but when we get the chance... that one shot to shine, we shine on to tell the world and open doors to the ones coming behind us." - Brandon Morris

_____
_____
_____
_____
_____
_____

Day 251

Winning comes as a result of preparation and the application of your objectives to reach your envisioned goals.

Day 252

"For our light affliction, which is but for a moment, worketh for us a far more exceeding *and* eternal weight of glory; while we look not at the things which are seen, but at the things which are not seen: for the things which are seen *are* temporal; but the things which are not seen *are* eternal." - II Corinthians 4:17-18

Day 253

To reach great levels of accomplishment requires great sacrifices over and over again.

Day 254

I will work on developing more patience so that I can learn to be stress free.

Day 255

What you failed to destroy will eventually destroy you.

Day 256

"If, before going to bed every night, you will tear a page from the calendar, and remark, 'there goes another day of my life, never to return,' you will become time conscious."

— A. B. Zu Tavern

Day 257

"When a man/woman's knowledge is not in order, the more of it he has the greater will be his/her confusion."
- Herbert Spencer

Day 258

The secret of your future is hidden in your daily routine.

Day 259

"And he said unto me, my grace is sufficient for thee: for my strength is made perfect in weakness. Most gladly therefore will I rather glory in my infirmities, that the power of Christ may rest upon me." - II Corinthians 12:9

_____
_____
_____
_____
_____
_____

Day 260

Get through the rough spots today by looking forward to the moment when you can say "All finished!"

_____
_____
_____
_____
_____
_____

Day 261

Do not give up after the first sign of trouble. Press on to your freedom.

Day 262

"I wanted to be scared again... I wanted to feel unsure again. That's the only way I learn, the only way I feel challenged." - Connie Chung

Day 263

"A man cannot discover new oceans unless he has the courage to lose sight of the shore." - Myles Munroe

_____
_____
_____
_____
_____
_____

Day 264

"The night is far spent, the day is at hand: let us therefore cast off the works of darkness, and let us put on the armor of light." - Romans 13:12

_____
_____
_____
_____
_____
_____

Day 265

"But he said, yea rather, blessed *are* they that hear the word of God, and keep it." - Luke 11:28

Day 266

"I never encouraged anyone to pray for a win. I don't think our players should be directed to the score of a game. That seems way too selfish. I wanted my teams to honor GOD by doing their best, controlling their emotions, and asking for protection. Those are the good requests for basketball players and for our lives in general." - John Wooden

Day 267

"Time is at once the most valuable and the most perishable of all our possessions." - John Randolph

---

Day 268

I must work on my mind, body, and spirit.

Day 269

Your transformation and change shall bring about divine direction.

Day 270

In due season always give what was so freely given to you. The more you give away the knowledge and wisdom of growth to others, the more you keep.

Finding Peace While in the Midst of the Storm

Day 271

"Give us help from trouble: for vain is the help of man."
                                                                                        - Psalm 105:12

Day 272

I will keep the reward of my freedom forever present in my mind.

Day 273

"And he said unto me, my grace is sufficient for thee: for my strength is made perfect in weakness. Most gladly therefore will I rather glory in my infirmities, that the power of Christ may rest upon me." - II Corinthians 12:9

_____
_____
_____
_____
_____
_____

Day 274

"Our business in life is not to get ahead of others, but to get ahead of ourselves - to break our own records, to outstrip our yesterday by our today." - Stewart B. Johnson

_____
_____
_____
_____
_____
_____

Day 275

"One who asks a question is a fool for five minutes; one who does not ask a question remains a fool forever."
 - Chinese proverb

Day 276

"Take my yoke upon you, and learn of me; for I am meek and lowly in heart: and ye shall find rest unto your souls"
 - Matthew 11:29

Day 277

I have found that being in any type of prison requires a commitment to becoming aware of the issues that caused the imprisonment in the first place. SELF AWARENESS.

Day 278

The first step to the road of rehabilitation is to examine yourself so that you can begin the process of redemption.

Day 279

"O Lord my God, in thee do I put my trust" - Psalm 7:1

Day 280

Never allow those things that are of no value to your growth to have your permission to cause you harm.

Day 281

Your life will be measured by the repeated actions of your daily efforts to attain success.

Day 282

No person wins a great task by themselves. Honor those who help you on this journey.

Day 283

Today you must remember the potential you have for greatness.

Day 284

Your thoughts today can be the beginning of your best tomorrow.

Day 285

Our potential is unlimited once we learn to research and validate our finding.

Day 286

All the knowledge in the world does a man no good unless he demonstrates a use of effort to attain his sought after goals.

Day 287

See the grace and mercy that you have been given and be mindful to return to others what has been given to you.

Day 288

Your faith, and trust in your hope, is the essence of your belief in your GOD given ability to reach unforeseen potential in your life.

Day 289

"If any man defile the temple of God, him shall God destroy; for the temple of God is holy, which temple ye are." - I Corinthians 3:17

Day 290

Never allow someone's label or name to dictate who you are as a person. You must know that you're not who you once were but who you are in your current state and mind set, a winner.

Day 291

Keep your focus on your thinking by not allowing yourself to give away your personal power to others.

Day 292

Don't allow yourself to get caught up complaining and wasting energy on things that you cannot control.

Day 293

"Striving for excellence motivates you; striving for perfection is demoralizing." - Harriet Braiker

_____
_____
_____
_____
_____
_____

Day 294

Be kind, fair, and unafraid to speak up when you see an injustice.

_____
_____
_____
_____
_____
_____

Day 295

"It's how we spend our time here and now that really matters. If you are fed up with the way you have come to interact with time, change it." - Wieder Marcia

Day 296

Remember to reflect on your progress every day. Take time to consider what you have achieved and where you are going.

Day 297

"Jesus said, 'I will not leave you comfortless: I will come to you.'" - John 14:18

Day 298

"An invasion of armies can be resisted, but not an invasion of ideals." - Victor Hugo

Day 299

"A man/woman is not old until regrets take the place of dreams." - John Barrymore

Day 300

Find your secret place to meditate and pray. Pray on those things that you desire to be better in.

Day 301

Lord, please give me the strength to stay in your will.

Day 302

"Tough times never last, but tough people do."
                              -Rev. Robert H Schuller

Day 303

"For the scripture saith, whosoever believeth on him shall not be ashamed." - Romans 10:11

Day 304

"Everyone thinks of changing the world, but no one thinks of changing himself." - Leo Tolstoy

Day 305

"You can't stop people from thinking, but you can start them." - Frank A. Dusch

Day 306

"A good man sheweth favour, and lendeth: He will guide his affairs with discretion." - Psalm 112:5

Day 307

We were put on earth to excel through the clouds and beyond.

Day 308

"A tree is known by its fruit; a man by his deeds. A good deed is never lost; he who sows courtesy reaps friendship, and he who plants kindness gathers love." - St. Basil

Day 309

One saint to another, be blessed with the Wisdom of Solomon, the leadership of Nehemiah, and the courage of Gideon.

Day 310

Speak and act with more enthusiasm.

Day 311

"For, he that expects nothing shall not be disappointed, but he that expects much—if he lives and uses that in hand day by day—shall be full to running over."

— Edgar Cayce

Day 312

"For me, winning isn't something that happens suddenly on the field when the whistle blows and the crowds roar. Winning is something that builds physically and mentally every day that you train and every night that you dream."

— Emmitt Smith

Day 313

"What lies behind us and what lies before us are tiny matters, compared to what lies within us."

— Oliver Wendell Holmes

Day 314

"It's simply a matter of doing what you do best and not worrying about what the other fellow is going to do."

— John R. Amos

Day 315

The foundation of all we do is built on giving back to others what was so freely given to us.

_____
_____
_____
_____
_____
_____

Day 316

"Let all things be done decently and in order."
- I Corinthians 14:40

_____
_____
_____
_____
_____
_____

Day 317

"When a man puts a limit on what he can be he has put a limit on what he will be." - Myles Munroe

_____
_____
_____
_____
_____

Day 318

"Your ability needs responsibility to expose its possibilities. Do what you can with what you have where you are."
— Theodore Roosevelt

_____
_____
_____
_____
_____

Day 319

It does not matter what you have been through, all that matters now is how you come through it.

Day 320

It doesn't matter anymore what happens. GOD has let me have a second chance to be found again. To be the man I was made to be.

Day 321

Gain the powerful surge of energy that accompanies a positive mental outlook.

_____
_____
_____
_____
_____
_____

Day 322

Stop a bad mood dead in its tracks, and turn it into "full speed ahead" positivity.

_____
_____
_____
_____
_____
_____

Day 323

"Jesus said, 'For I say unto you, that except your righteousness shall exceed the righteousness of the scribes and Pharisees, ye shall in no case enter into the kingdom of heaven.'" - Matthew 5:20

Day 324

"Jesus said, 'Take heed to yourselves: If thy brother trespass against thee, rebuke him; and if he repent, forgive him.'" - Luke 17:3

Day 325

"The most important of life's battles is the one we fight daily in the silent chambers of the soul." - David McKay

_____
_____
_____
_____
_____
_____

Day 326

"We must accept finite disappointment, but never lose infinite hope." - Martin Luther King Jr.

_____
_____
_____
_____
_____
_____

Day 327

"Motivation is like food for the brain. You cannot get enough in one sitting. It needs continual and regular top ups." - Peter Davies

Day 328

"Part of being a champ is acting like a champ. You have to learn how to win and not run away when you lose. Everyone has bad stretches and real successes. Either way, you have to be careful not to lose your confidence or get too confident." - Nancy Kerrigan

Day 329

"The fight is won or lost far away from witnesses - behind the lines, in the gym, and out there on the road, long before I dance under those lights." - Muhammad Ali

Day 330

"No one can make you feel inferior without your consent."
- Eleanor Roosevelt

Day 331

"Opportunities are usually disguised as hard work, so most people don't recognize them." - Ann Landers

---

Day 332

"Use what you've been through as fuel, believe in yourself and be unstoppable!" – Yvonne Pierre

Day 333

"There is great treasure there behind our skull and this is true about all of us. This little treasure has great, great powers, and I would say we only have learned a very, very small part of what it can do." - Isaac Bashevis Singer

Day 334

"Without goals, and plans to reach them, you are like a ship that has set sail with no destination."

- Fitzhugh Dodson

Day 335

"Some self-confronting questions: Where do I want to be at any given time? How am I going to get there? What do I have to do to get myself from where I am to where I want to be? What's the first, small step I can take to get moving?" - George A. Ford

Day 336

Your work and effort must be focused so that your outcome and results equal your day one goals.

Day 337

"Jesus said, 'If ye abide in me, and my words abide in you, ye shall ask what ye will, and it shall be done unto you.'" - John 15:7

Day 338

"The beginning is the most important part of the work."
- Plato

Day 339

Never sleeping, only resting, I will sleep when I die. I got to go get it because nobody will do it for me.

Day 340

"The world cares very little about what a man or woman knows; it is what a man or woman is able to do that counts." - Booker T. Washington

Day 341

I will praise GOD in the midst of the storm ... You ask me why? It's like this; I know GOD has considered me, to be the one to endure this storm.

Day 342

Do whatever it takes positively to keep the dream alive.

Day 343

I see people being so easily detoured from their dream because of this or that situation. You have to be an overcomer, stop complaining about not getting the best possible situation there is. Make it become YOUR best situation. Great things and success do not come easily without sacrificing something.

Day 344

Lift up the spirits and inspire others when they are down.

Day 345

Say "YES!" to each new challenge as it presents itself.

Day 346

The power of accountability is the key to your freedom.

Day 347

"All men are sent to the world with limitless credit, but few draw to their full extent." - Myles Munroe

Day 348

"Courage is fear that has said its prayers." - Karl Barth

Day 349

"Success seems to be connected with action. Successful people keep moving. They make, mistakes, but they don't quit." - Conrad Hilton

Day 350

With each awakening there is an opportunity to be successful.

Day 351

Until you learn to serve yourself the good things of life you're giving is in vain.

Day 352

Every struggle in life is the beginning of your testimony of being able to show someone the hope in change.

Day 353

"Those who profess to love freedom and yet deprecate agitation are those who want crops without plowing. This struggle may be a moral one, or it may be physical, but it must be a struggle. Power concedes nothing without a demand. It never did, and it never will."

- Fredrick Douglass

Day 354

We never have to walk alone if we walk with GOD.

Day 355

This is the moment to look back at where all the hard work has gotten you so far. Stand still and look back over the road you have traveled only for a moment.

_____
_____
_____
_____
_____
_____

Day 356

Keep the mind productive and you will reap the rewards of an intellectual harvest.

_____
_____
_____
_____
_____
_____

Day 357

See beyond your current circumstance and find the solution to your present problems.

Day 358

Food for thought... Never have a celebration for a guy coming home from prison with alcohol and drugs. The alcohol and drugs may lead to him going back to prison. Find other ways to help celebrate his freedom.

Day 359

I wish I could share this moment with you all; how good God has been to me and how much I feel so blessed to know that God loves me enough to have allowed me to accomplish all the things. He has allowed me to accomplish. I am truly experiencing a second chance - redeemed, found again and standing large.

Day 360

You're never too old to make the sacrifices and take the risks to be an example to others and to inspire children.

Day 361

When I stop and think of the goodness of God my heart is overwhelmed and what He has done for me. I can't help but cry when I think about how HE spared my life. He gave me a new life and a second chance to be something other than what I was. Glory Hallelujah.

Day 362

I shall allow God to do his work through me so that I can have a testimony to give my children. Thank you Jesus!!!

Day 363

"Jesus said unto him, 'If thou canst believe, all things *are* possible to him that believeth.'" - Mark 9:23

Day 364

By age 35, I had spent 18 years in jails and prison. Between incarcerations, I had been shot nine times. Drugs and crime were my life, and I saw no reason to change. But, because of my relationship with God, and the miracles that He has given me, I have come this far and cannot turn around now.

Day 365

"Jesus said, 'and I will give unto thee the keys of the kingdom of heaven: and whatsoever thou shalt bind on earth shall be bound in heaven: and whatsoever thou shalt loose on earth shall be loosed in heaven.'"

- Matthew 16:19

Letters to Mr. Moore

Dear Mr. Moore,

This is a thank you letter from me to you for all your knowledge and wisdom you have gave and share with me and others in the Living Free Program. I've been here in this program for the last five months. I made it in the graduation. I just want to say how much I appreciate and I'm very grateful to you, Mr. Williams, Dick, Vickie, Mary Ann, and Bishop Smith for everything you have done for me and others. You have paved the road of recovery for me and have given me these precision tools to work with to give me a brand new start in life that I now have a new beginning with relationships with myself, my family, my finance and my co-workers on my job. I plan to stay clean and sober. And continue to work my program after I am release soon. I am a true believer in Christ. I'm renewing my relation with the Lord. I have picked up my cross and will continue to follow Jesus. We know we all are in the middle of a spiritual warfare. Therefore, I know what I must do and continue to fight the good fight of faith. I plan to keep in contact with you and the others. You have been a very powerful and positive role model. Thanks for your help. Peace

- Yours truly

Tony,

I wanted to say thank you for all of the encouragement and knowledge you have given me over the past 9 months. I am really grateful for the Living Free Program. I have learned so from you about myself through the Cognitive Thinking Patterns. I never realized what I was doing but now understand the mistakes I have made and that exist in my life. I don't know my future but I know that with faith I can make it. I look forward to contacting you if and when I do get out. You are a very positive role model and inspiration for me. GOD Bless.

Mr. Moore,

On behalf of myself and the A.O.D.A group I would like to thank you for coming to share a part of your life with us. We know that you're a busy person so we appreciate that time you took out to do so.
I got a lot out of your talk mainly the part on where I have to be a good man and not poison myself, my child's mother, my child or those that are around me. I have to take a leader's stand point and show good things for not only myself but for those around me and I know it can only start from within me. I just have to have the drive, determination and discipline for the course.
Thank You

Tony Moore,

I'm writing to say thank you for coming and sharing your story about how you change your life around after you got out of prison. It shows me that people can make it and not just talk about it. I have two kids both boys and they are the reason why I'm changing my life around and going to make better choices than what I use to make. I took one of your cards to keep in contact if I have a problem with something. I live in La Crosse but I'm willing to drive to Kenosha and hear you speak and sit in on one of the meetings.

Thank you again Tony Moore

Dear Tony Moore,

Thank you for coming in and sharing your life story with us. It's good to hear it from a person who actually lived it. I also struggle with a drug addiction and hearing your story gives me hope. You showed me that it is possible as long as I'm dedicated. Thank you for taking the time to come and speak to us.

Thank You

To Birds of a Feather,

In November of 2007, I got out of RCI. I had a drug problem and alcohol addiction. I have done drugs and drank my whole life. I have been through Options in 2000-2001. I stopped for a while but continued to smoke pot and drink. In June of 07 my P.O. put me in jail then in prison. Then November 07 that's when I started Birds of a Feather Group on Monday and Fridays. This time I really wanted the help to stop screwing up my life. My wife and family have been through enough. 40 years of problems took its toll. Most of all I had do it for me. The help I got from Tony and everyone else, I started to put to my everyday life. I started to think before I acted. I thought of the (consequences) troubles. I made the right decisions for me. I learned that I can live a better life being sober. I have money in the bank, I have a house, new truck and most of all I have a healthy body. Well, at least well than I had before. The main thing I learned most of all is you have to want to do it. (Be Clean)

Thank you very much, Tony and everyone

Dear Mr. Moore,

I want to thank you for taking the time out of your schedule to come and share your life with young men in a situation such as ours. It shows care and concern for our generation and I appreciate that. Your time spent speaking was very informative. The things you touched bases on were some things that we needed to be warned about so that we may avoid them. And the other things were things that are applicable to take the steps toward succeeding in a legal fashion. So I thank you for your information and I'm glad we heard what we heard from someone who has had hands on experience with the subjects brought up. So thank you for coming and congratulations on your success and May GOD bless.

Thankfully

Tony,

Thank you for coming in to speak. Your presentation made an impact on me because you went through a lot of thing I did. So I see that I can do a positive thing when I get out. How you made a change was good. So for myself I learned a lot from your presentation. I like what you spoke of when you said to build yourself up when someone tries to break you down. I liked your presentation you did a good job.

Thank you

Tony,

Thank you for taking the time out of your busy work day to assist me further on our journey to help the unsheltered home throughout the United States as well as Kenosha. With Gratitude and special sincere thanks. Thank you so much. It's the little acts of kindness that means so very much.
Your thoughtfulness was appreciated more than words can say.

Tony,

Thanks for a job well done in class. My favorite was when you told us to take a look in the mirror and ask how did I get here?! The reason it impacted me, was I did that. I think that was the worst pain I ever experienced, however the outcome was the greatest joy because that was my day of deliverance. So as I did my soul search "GOD" was also giving me a hug. You can say "GOD" gave me an intervention with a hug and delivered me in 2006.

Thanks

Dear Tony Moore,

Hopefully this letter will find you in the best of health and still doing for others what you have done for me. I mainly would just like to convey onto you and Bishop what is going on with me at this time. I have maintained acceptable institution behavior and I just recently attended a graduation ceremony for the Microsoft computer program that I completed.

Please be advised that upon my release I will still be seeking the help and consultation of Birds of a Feather and from Bishop as well. I would greatly appreciate it if I am still welcomed to come and get what the two of you have to offer. I am intelligent enough to know that I need it. Please be so kind as to pass this onto Bishop.

This time last year you and I were together by means of K.C.D.C and Living Free. Wow have time flew by. I am no longer at K.C.D.C., but I want to forever be a part of the living that is mentally and physically free. I am unable to express to you enough of me wanting the help of you and Bishop to ensure that I remain that way.

Thank you for your time and attention

Tony Moore